Aphorisms for Thirsty Fish

The Lost Writings of Wu Hsin, Vol. 1

Translation by Roy Melvyn

Aphorisms for Thirsty Fish
The Lost Writings of Wu Hsin, Vol. 1
Translation by Roy Melvyn
Copyright 2011 Roy Melvyn

Summa Iru Publishing
Boulder, Colorado 80020

Brief Background

It is widely believed that Wu Hsin was born during the Warring States Period (403-221 BCE), postdating the death of Confucius by more than one hundred years.

This was a period during which the ruling house of Zhou had lost much of its authority and power, and there was increasing violence between states. This situation birthed "the hundred schools", the flourishing of many schools of thought, each setting forth its own concepts of the prerequisites for a return to a state of harmony. The two most influential schools were that of Confucius and the followers of Mozi ("Master Mo"), the Mohists. The latter were critical of the elitist nature and extravagant behaviors of the traditional culture. The philosophical movement associated with the Daodejing also was emerging at this time. Wu Hsin's style of Daoist philosophy developed within the context defined by these three schools and appears to be most heavily influenced by that latter. In addition, it most clearly contains the seeds of what would become Ch'an Buddhism in China or Zen in Japan.

Wu Hsin was born in a village called Meng, in the state of Song. The Pu River in which Wu Hsin was said to have fished was in the state of Chen which had become a territory of Chu. We might say that Wu Hsin was situated in the borderlands between Chu and the central plains—the plains centered around the Yellow River which were the home of the Shang and Zhou cultures. Certainly, as one learns more about the culture of Chu, one senses deep resonances with the aesthetic sensibility of the Daoists, and with Wu Hsin's style in particular.

If the traditional dating is reliable, Wu Hsin would have been a contemporary of Mencius, but one is hard pressed to find any evidence that there was any communication between them. The philosopher Gao Ming, although not a Daoist, was a close friend and stories abound of their philosophical rivalries.

Wu Hsin's work was significant for Daoist religious practitioners who often took ideas and themes from it for their meditation practice, as an example, Sima Chengzhen's 'Treatise on Sitting and Forgetting' (ca. 660 C.E.).

He offers a highly refined view of life and living. When he writes "Nothing appears as it seems", he challenges the reader to question and verify every belief and every assumption.

Brevity was the trademark of his writing style. Whereas his contemporaries were writing lengthy tomes, Wu Hsin's style reflected his sense that words, too, were impediments to the attainment of Understanding; that they were only pointers and nothing more. He would use many of the same words over and over because he felt that people needed to hear words repeatedly, until the Understanding was louder than the words.

His writings are filled with paradoxes, which cause the mind to slow down and, at times, to even stop. Reading Wu Hsin, one must ponder. However, it is not an active pondering, but a passive one, much in the same way as one puts something in the oven and lets it bake for a while.

He repeatedly returns to three key points. First, on the phenomenal plane, when one ceases to resist What-Is and becomes more in harmony with It, one attains a state of Ming, or clear seeing. Having arrived at this point, all action becomes wei wu wei, or action without action (non-forcing) and there is a working in harmony with What-Is to accomplish what is required.

Second, as the clear seeing deepens (what he refers to as the opening of the great gate), the understanding arises that there is no one doing anything and that there is only the One doing everything through the many and diverse objective phenomena which serve as Its instruments.

From this flows the third and last: the seemingly separate me is a misapprehension, created by the mind which divides everything into pseudo-subject (me) and object (the world outside of this me). This seeming two-ness (dva in Sanskrit, duo in Latin, dual in English), this feeling of being separate and apart, is the root cause of unhappiness.

The return to wholeness is nothing more than the end of this division. It is an apperception of the unity between the noumenal and the phenomenal in much the same way as there is a single unity between the sun and sunlight. Then, the pseudo-subject is finally seen as only another object while the true Subjectivity exists prior to the arising of both and is their source.

All five volumes consist of what would appear to be his day-to-day reflections as they spontaneously arose. There is no progression in the pages, no evolution of the concepts put forth. As such, reading pages randomly or from the beginning has the same efficacy. Nor should it be read with haste; a page or two at a time is sufficient to allow for the content to sink in, as a thrown stone falls to the bottom of the lake.

In its essence, this book is a collection of hooks; any one of them is sufficient to catch a thirsty fish

Translator's Note

Material of this nature is not served well by language. It may seem that there are anomalies and contradictions. So, it is important to state that the translation of Wu Hsin's words herein is not purely literal. Instead, it contains an interpretation of what was clearly implied, and this is where the limitation of words is quite evident.

Compounding this problem, I have chosen to incorporate certain words into the translation which may appear to be incongruent relative to the time of Wu Hsin's writing.

The clearest example of this would be my use of the word ego which wasn't to come into being for many of hundreds of years after Wu Hsin's death.

I have done this to best capture the real essence of the intention behind the word. The original Chinese word 个人 (ge ren) means the individual. However, using the individual doesn't capture the sense of separateness that is better conveyed by ego.

The Sanskrit language also provides us with some marvelous insight. In it, the word for mind is manas, which translated literally means that which measures and compares. That says it pretty well. The Sanskrit word for ego is ahamkara; its translation is *I am the doer*. Within the context of Wu Hsin's message, the conveyance of the idea of I am the doer is vitally important. As such, this and other small liberties that I have taken with the translation feel more than reasonable.

RM

Aphorisms for Thirsty Fish

Text

What follows is
A dissertation on the Unspeakable.
It is an attempt to
Describe the Undescribable;
To capture with words
That which cannot be captured;
The Unutterable.
As such, it is destined to fall short.
That having been said,
Let us now proceed.

These words are
The transmission of Wu Hsin.
Thanks be to Heaven for
Granting their approval.
They transcend time and
Therefore are beyond time.
They will be as valid in
Five thousand years as
They are in this moment.
In the absence of a resonance,
They will have no meaning nor
Create any interest.
This resonance cannot be willed into being.
It is either inherent by nature or
It is not.
These words come out from
A place devoid of
Concepts and doubts.
As such, they are not only spontaneous, but
Natural and true.
They are not intended to
Create new concepts,
But, to instead,
Dispel old ones.
The words of Wu Hsin are
Not meant for discussion which only
Distorts and pollutes.
Take them in and
Move on.

This is the present condition:
Birth is the entry to phenomenality.
Death is the exit from phenomenality.
All that requires insight is:
Who is born and who dies?
Or better stated:
What is born and what dies?

*****

The attachment to beliefs is
The greatest shackle.
To be free is
To know that
One does not know.

*****

One is what
One absorbs

*****

It is easier to teach a blind man
To paint than it is
To convey What-Is with mere words.

The end of questioning is
The same as
The end of seeking.
Further and further explanations
Do not provide
That which is sought.
Additional information
Does not provide
That which is sought.
Drop these activities and
Rest in what is
Prior to all mental activity:
Awareness.

*****

Sound is the same but
Its expression
Through various instruments is different.
So it is with Being.

*****

Half knowledge cannot take one
To full wisdom.
Knowledge of the world is inferior to
Knowledge of that which
Births the world and is
Prior to it.

*****

What problems can there be that
The mind did not create?
The solution to problems begins with
The cessation in believing in
The content of one's thoughts.

To know that one is, is natural.
To know what one is
Requires a diving into the depths of
One's own being.
The pearl rests on the bottom.

*****

An event becomes
An experience through
Personal involvement.
Collecting experiences can be
Helpful with the daily aspects of life,
But it is not
The road to happiness.

*****

It is understood that
Sleep is the desire for
A period of rest
For the body.
It is less understood that
Sleep is the desire for
A period of rest
Away from the body.

*****

The inherent nature of mind is
To process thought.
To attempt the cessation of thought
Goes against what is natural.
The goal, therefore, is not
The cessation of thought.
The goal is cessation of
Identification with thought.

All this running around,
Praying and making offerings so that
The next life will be better than
This life.
What silliness!
Life after this death is
Not different than,
Nor better than
Life before this birth.

*****

At the root,
There is no difference between
Separation and dissatisfaction.
This is so because
Feeling separate and apart is
The primary dissatisfaction.

*****

Thoughts intrude, like
Unwelcome guests at a party.
Ignored and unfed,
They depart.

*****

What is called peace by many is
Merely the absence of disturbance.
True peace cannot be disturbed;
It resides beyond the reach of disturbance.

Nothing is as it seems.
The common view is that
There is a subjective observer
Observing an objective world;
The former separate from
The latter.
Nothing is as it seems.

*****

When here becomes
Everywhere and
Now becomes
Always, then
One has succeeded.

*****

When one is enthralled with
The beauty on the surface of the ocean,
The immensity of its depths can
Never be discerned.

The Source and Substance of everything
Has no name.
When Wu Hsin names it:
The Eternal or
The Infinite or
What-Is or
That or
The Mystery or
The Absolute,
He merely points to It.
Make a list of
All your pains,
Your sorrows,
Your hurts and disappointments.
This, too, is
Part of It.

*****

There is reading
But no reader of this writing
Without an author.
The merger of
The reading and the writing is
Deep insight and understanding.

*****

How many have there been
Who have come to Wu Hsin
To ask "Why?"
Why is this? or
Why is that?
"Why?"
As there are many perspectives,
There can be many answers.
Yet, in the end,
The best answer to "Why?" is
Why not?

It is man
Who is in movement
Against the background of immobility.
But who moves the moved?

*****

We are afloat in
The Great River.
All are carried along.
Some swim against the flow.
They, too, are carried along.

*****

The departure from what is natural is
The birthplace of personality.
The world of persons is
A solitary place,
Each separate and alone.
To achieve peace,
One must retrace the way one came.

*****

What is latent and
What is dormant are
Not the same.
The dormant arises and sets;
The latent ever is.

Only the fool
Seeks to stop
The shaking of
The moon's reflection on the water.
The acceptance of what
Cannot be changed
Paves the way to
The changeless.

*****

All of the world, with its
Past, present and future,
Arises every morning and
Sets every night,
To arise again the next day.
The knower of this has moved
Out of involvement and
Into the understanding that
In order for this world to be known,
The knower must precede it.

*****

The one who considers himself
To be free
Is free.
The one who considers himself
To be bound
Is bound.
The only prison is mental.

*****

Wu Hsin has no sumptuous buffet
Presented on a silver platter.
The offering is basic fare,
To be eaten and fully savored.
Then, there is nothing remaining
For one to do.

Controlling the mind doesn't
Take one to freedom.
Controlling the mind
Adds another link
To one's shackles.

*****

Regardless of how fast one runs
There is no escape
From oneself.
The impetus of this escape is
This state which is
Believed to be unsatisfactory.
To succeed, one must relinquish
The smaller for
The greater.

*****

Whereas pain is
A physical experience
Suffering is a mental one.
It is the sense that
Things should be
Other than they are.
Its antidote is
Acceptance.

The trance of separateness is
The jail.
The imagination is
The jailer.
When one no longer believes
What one imagines oneself to be,
The cell door opens and
The realization dawns that
A life filled up with being somebody is
An empty existence.

*****

When the waterwheel stops turning,
What happens to
The energy that turned it?
Is it said to be used up or
That it remains dormant,
To turn again?
When the body dies,
What dies and
What goes on?
That which animated the body
Ceases to do so.
This That is not affected and
The cycle continues.

*****

Gods and their universes
Come and go.
Avatars appear in unceasing succession.
In the end, that which was present
At the beginning
Remains.

Instead of scurrying here and there,
Man must stabilize in
That which supports him.
Once stabilized,
All scurrying becomes
Spontaneous and appropriate.

*****

The reformation of others
Must not take precedence over
The reformation of oneself.
Reforming oneself requires
The remembrance of the days
Prior to which
One became an individual.

*****

Solitude is not
A condition of the body.
Instead, it is
A condition of the mind.
Solitude may be found
In the busy market or
May be elusive in the forest.

*****

Do no mistake
The five points of a star
For five stars.
All there is
Is a single, unitary
Everything.

The seeker of union
Must admit separation.
For the knower of union,
There is nothing to do.

*****

There is no difference between
That which dwells
Within a sparrow and
That which dwells in
The body of man.
Two instruments;
One large,
The other small.

*****

The best altar has
Nothing on it.

*****

What Wu Hsin says
Requires no explanation.
Explanation requires concepts and
Cogitation.
That is not the way.
Wu Hsin plants the seed in the soil;
It grows at its own pace.

Openness has no location in particular.
It contains everything.
It contains thoughts and
The absence of thoughts.
It contains feelings and no feelings,
Sights and no sights,
Sounds and silence.
Within openness,
Everything is invited and
Everything is accepted.
There is no way
To be open because
There is no difference between
Being open and
Being.

*****

In human beings,
There is a need
To create order
Out of what is
Perceived to be chaos.
This ordering mechanism is
The mind.
As such, the mind seeks causes
To explain what it
Doesn't understand.
Is the carrot the cause of the chicken soup
Or is it the chicken
Or is it the broth
Or is it the cook?
With the apperception that
Everything is perfect as it is, that
Everything causes everything else,
The mind, as fixer,
As judge,
As organizer,
Loses its relevance.

Words are the net used
To capture the world.
Mind is the means used
To devour the world.
Both fail;
Can the wind be kept in
A box?
Truth is halved when
It is told.

*****

A common misconception is
The belief that thinking is
The creation of thought.
Rather, it is
The reception of thought from
A source which has no name and
From a place that cannot be found.
Since one can't decide to think
Nor can one decide
Thoughts' contents,
Why does one
Claim their ownership?
Is every sound Wu Hsin's because
He can hear them?

*****

Do not come to Wu Hsin as if
To a tailor
With an order for a garment where
The style, fabric and measurements
Are all predetermined and acceptable.
Rather, desire to come away nude;
Denuded of concepts, beliefs and
All ideations.

The personality is like
A unique color.
When its work is done,
It returns to the colorless
From where it emerged.

*****

Do not become preoccupied with
What occurs after death unless
There is willingness to die today.
This death, which is only
The death of identification, is
The doorway to liberation.

*****

Immanence,
Intemporal
Impersonal and
Infinite
Is the canvas
On which the world
Appears and disappears.
Drops on a canvas,
Nothing more is
Man .

All men are seekers from birth.
First, they seek to suck
From their mother's breast.
Later, they seek wealth or fame
Or security
Or power
Or love
Or peace.
Seeking itself is
The fundamental condition of the world and
The seeker is merely the instrument
Through which it occurs.

*****

Let us go upstream
For a moment
To a place before
You and me;
Before
All you's and all me's.
This place is called
Beginning.
Empty, yet full
Of potential,
It is from here that
All emerges.

*****

Here is the utter
Simplicity of the matter:
In the absence of identification
With any thing,
Who are you?
Or better still,
What are you?

The sight of the face of
Your god
Continues to be elusive.
How can the Formless,
That pervades every aspect of
Every thing,
Be seen
Or heard
Or smelled
Or touched
Or tasted?
At the core, Wu Hsin asks:
How is immanence discerned?
The answer is known to those
Who understand that
There is no difference
Between the substance and
That which animates it.

*****

The Ultimate Understanding is
An impersonal event
Occurring in phenomenality.
As such, there is no need for you,
Or any you
To be concerned about it.
Go about your business and
Enjoy life.

*****

For many,
The first step on
A spiritual journey is to
Become lost.
The final step is
Losing one's self.

To draw water from this well
Called Wu Hsin,
One must bring a bucket and
Ten feet of rope.
Most arrive with eight feet of rope,
Then leave,
Believing the well to be dry.
It is as it is.

*****

Life is experienced
As a series of events
Happening to an individual.
Wu Hsin says:
Life is happening.
The individual is merely
One of the series
Of events.

*****

Chasing after the things
One yearns for is
Inferior to
Chasing after
The source of the yearning.

*****

The entire universe is
The teacher
If one is willing to end
The entrancement with
The momentary.
Lessons then become boundless.

Ebbing begins when
Tides are at their highest.
When the unbearable is recognized
To be bearable,
Profound transformation occurs.

*****

How can it be otherwise?
Perfection contains all
Imperfection;
The smaller within the larger.
Do not chastise your gods
For the aspects of life deemed
Unacceptable.

*****

To search for happiness
Implies its absence.
This implication is a fundamental flaw.
Happiness is ever present.
It may become obscured,
Such obscuration being temporary.

*****

All experience is like an echo,
Occurring after the event and
Distorting it by varying degrees.
The distance between the event and
The experience is directly related to
The scale of involvement of
The experiencer.

Infancy comes, then
Childhood and adulthood
Followed by middle age and lastly,
Old age.
All these stages come and go upon
That which is immovable.

*****

Viewed through the lens of time,
Many important things are
Rendered unimportant.

*****

Although a mouse in a well
Knows nothing about
The sparrows in the sky,
In the moment of its escape
Everything changes.

*****

The preoccupation with
The foreground, the sights,
The smells,
The sounds,
Takes the attention away from
The background.
Yet, it is in this very background that
The Mystery resides.

When there is no inside,
No outside,
No top,
No bottom,
No breadth,
No width,
No surface and
No depth, then
There is only here and
There is no place else to go.

*****

One is carried on a raft
Within a floating stream.
One is neither the raft nor
The stream yet
The perceiver of both.

*****

What is natural
Follows no laws nor
Requires any.
Can there be a rule for
The beating of the heart or
The blackness of the raven?
There is a natural rhythm to
The workings of the world.
Some are discernable
While others cannot be discerned.
It is the dance
Between the two that
Creates action.

*****

Trust that what brought you here
Will take you there.

The Infinite has no preferences.
It kisses both the darkness and
The light equally.

*****

Wu Hsin speaks of only
One thing, and that
One thing is
Everything.
As soon as the speaking begins,
There is movement away from It.
Words reduce the incomprehensible into
Something more digestible.

*****

Contrary to popular belief
The perceiver and that
Which is perceived are
Two ends of
The same stick.
The absence of one is
The absence of both.
The absence of everything
Uncovers the presence of
The Seed of everything.

*****

Whatever has been clung to as myself
Disappears in the course of time.
Yet, what has been steady throughout, is
Overlooked.

Many writings speak of
The Creator.
Yet, in truth,
This Creator is only
Another creation.
Who created
The Creator?

*****

What begins as a crack
Becomes a window
Then a door
Until the entire structure vanishes.
Wu Hsin calls this
The unfolding of awareness.

*****

There is no forest,
There is no cave,
There is no mountaintop
Where one can hide
From oneself.

*****

One cannot acquire true knowledge and
Maintain a hold on ignorance.
The two are mutually exclusive.
Release of the latter is
A precondition for the
Arrival of the former.

When vision and compassion
Expand to include the opposition,
The opposition ceases to oppose.

*****

Slow ripening and rapid flowering
Alternate.
One is not superior to the other.
Be not concerned with pace,
Be concerned with depth.
Worries about progress are for children.

*****

All there is is consciousness.
Consciousness is all there is.
In the absence of consciousness,
What is there?
All manifestation
Appears in consciousness
Disappears in consciousness.
Consciousness is the precondition for
All perception.
Everything perceived
Is perceived
By consciousness as
An object in consciousness,
Including the perceiver.
Understand this and
Then grow your carrots.

Wu Hsin requires that
One question those things that are
Not open to question.
These are the rocks to which
One's feet are tied.

*****

All experiences are transitory.
The wise man neither seeks nor
Rejects them.
In this manner,
One remains rooted in
The Unchanging,
The stage upon which
All change occurs.
For many,
What they believe to be
Their castle, is in fact
Their jail.
The addiction to the drug called intellect,
Results in analysis of everything.
All this perusal,
Evaluation and
Analysis complicates
What is simple.
Becoming purely receptive
Strips away the false,
Leaving the great gate to open, then
What-Is is clearly comprehended.

*****

The greatest enjoyment is experienced
When there is no concern for its duration.

When there is indifference to outcomes,
One is willing to work with
Less than ideal means and
Postponement is avoided.

*****

Utilizing the mind in the attempt to
Achieve Ultimate Understanding is
Akin to hiring a thief to
Protect a house from burglars.

*****

Man can do
Whatever he wants.
However, he cannot
Will whatever he wants.

*****

Your reading these words
Is evidence enough to Wu Hsin that
The hook is already
In the fish's mouth.
I cannot tell you
How long it will take
To reel it in.
Most fight,
Some do not.
In the end,
All come into my net.

Shadows working on shadows,
Seeking to comprehend the
Inconceivable immensity that is
What-Is.
Better it would be to
Simply enjoy oneself,
Doing what one is moved to do.

*****

If heat and cold
Comprise temperature and
Tall and short together
Comprise height,
Do subject and object comprise
The sum of life,
The perceiver and the perceived?

*****

Suppression is a lack of acceptance,
An attempt to nullify what is natural.
The treatment of symptoms
Does not cure the disease.
Effects vanish when
Causes are removed,
Not when they are suppressed.

The deep secret is that
You are beyond time,
Beyond the heavens.
You contact each at two points:
Here and Now.
Wu Hsin knows this,
You do not.
As such, you see yourself
As separate from the Totality
When, in fact,
You are the very Totality
You feel separate from.
Change your viewpoint and
Change the world.
Just as the eye
Cannot see itself,
The mind
Cannot know itself.
As such, all knowing
Must spring from that which is vaster.

*****

To dig a hole,
One employs a shovel.
When the hole is completed,
The grip on the shovel is released.
In order to teach,
Concepts must be used.
Once the teaching is assimilated,
The grip on the concept must be released.

When the need for action
Reaches an appropriate crescendo,
Action occurs.
This is the nature of
The world.
The one who
Performs the action is only
The instrument of action,
Nothing more.

*****

The only wisdom
One can acquire here is
The full apperception of
Who is the acquirer.
All else is like
Asking an unmarried man if
He has stopped
Beating his wife.

*****

The sum of a past is
I was.
The sum of a future is
I will be.
The continuous crossing back and forth
Between the two
Obscures the present moment,
The I am,
Being Itself.

*****

The empty cup
Has emptiness inside.
Wu Hsin asks:
What happens to the emptiness
When the cup is smashed?

The dawning of a willingness
To accept the unacceptable.
Produces the cessation of worry.
In a world without worry,
The empty man is an emperor.

*****

You have an image of
What this outcome should be.
I say to you:
Drop it.
There is no standard,
No bellwether,
By which to measure.
The appearance is of
No importance.
All that can be said is
You will recognize the unity
Prior to all appearance.

*****

To grow is necessary.
To outgrow is, likewise,
Necessary.

*****

Wu Hsin does not speak
In hypotheses.
It is the direct experience
Of What-Is that is conveyed.
The fact that
Words and concepts are
The pointers to this are
The inherent limitation
In all communication.

All emotions come and go
You remain.

                    *****

Your sack of concepts
Compels you
To see things
In a prescribed manner.
Dropping this sack
Allows your eyes to open and
For clarity to manifest.

                    *****

All your goodness,
All your years of practice,
All the prayers you have spoken,
Mean little to Wu Hsin.
Instead, tell me if
You are prepared to relinquish
The control that you exercise
On every aspect of your life?
Are you now ready
To enter into the flow of life
Without the oar of your seeming will?

                    *****

A free man's life is
A life that is free of
Demands,
Free of dependency.
With nothing to drag along
One goes where one will.

Why is there so much
Struggling with the practices,
Techniques and
Methods that are
Alleged to end all struggling?

*****

The groundless expanse is
Unknown territory.
Men prefer what is known,
Regardless of whether it is
Painful or pleasant.
Because there is nowhere
To hide in the vastness and
There is no place to run to,
The choice seems simple.
Yet, it is the very unwillingness
To embrace the unknown
That keeps it in the shadows.

*****

Is the perceiver
Separate from that which
Is perceived?
Tell Wu Hsin:
What is it that sees my knee
When I gaze upon my lap?

*****

What is the world?
The world is the sum of the known
Embraced by the fullness of
The unknown and
Protected by that which is
Unknowable.

When the mind feasts,
True knowledge is lost.
When the mind eats not,
True knowledge manifests.

*****

The experience of
The Mystery is the banter of fools.
Only objects,
Overt or subtle, are experienced,
While the Mystery is prior
To all objects.

*****

You are a sinner,
You are a saint.
You are a murderer and
You are a monk.
The entire world that
You experience is
Inside yourself.
To fix the problems of
The world,
You need only
Fix yourself.

*****

Where is the line
Of demarcation
That separates heaven
From this life?
Can you show it to me?
Does it exist at all, anywhere,
Aside from inside your head?

Do not come to Wu Hsin
So that your questions may be answered.
Do so in order that
Your answers may be questioned.

*****

All that is required
Is Understanding.
Not an understanding of things but
An Understanding of
The Potential of All Possibilities
That is prior to things.
Understand this and
You understand all.

*****

You came to this life
With your own unique nature.
It was combined with
The experiences you had
To forge who you are.
You had no say in the matter.
You are a one-of-a-kind instrument
Performing the work that
Only you can
In the service of That which
Sent you.

*****

What can you really
Claim to be yours
When it can be taken,
In the time it takes
To snap a finger,
By the One who
Gave it to you?

My father is
This-Now-Here;
My mother is
This-Now-Here;
My brother is
This-Now-Here;
My neighbor is
This-Now-Here;
All related.
When each is gone,
What endures?
This-Now-Here.
Thoughts are only
Puffs of smoke
Rising from the chimney of the mind.
Attaching attention to them is
The heart of suffering.

*****

What one really is
Is what one is
In the absence of
The who that
One thinks one is.

*****

There is no requirement to
Transcend the past.
All that must be done is to
Stop carrying it,
Like a block of stone,
On one's back.

Man is ensnared
In the continuum called Past-Future.
His attention remains fixated there,
Uninterrupted.
To free oneself from the trap,
Even for a single instant,
Return to the point of presence,
Of being.
Of being no thing in particular.
In this moment.
Then, miraculously,
The snare dissolves.

*****

Do not mistake
A mere rearranging of the furniture
For true change.

*****

Thinking creates more problems
Than it solves.

*****

Do not look for It
In moving water.
Moving water distorts.
Look for It
In still water.
Still water reflects perfectly.

There is great joy when
The raindrop is reunited with
The ocean.
Likewise, there is great joy
In death.
What dies, other than
A story filled with much sorrow and
Intermittent joy?

*****

Know Wu Hsin as
The Untouched.
Unaffected by time or
Space or
People or
Places or
Things,
Wu Hsin is not
While all else is moving.

*****

All doing is contained
In being.
When the attention is shifted from
Doing to being,
The doing takes care of itself
Without any intended doing and
In the absence of a doer.

What is it
That brings people to
The doorstep of Wu Hsin?
It is simply the desire
To know this What.
When Wu Hsin says
This What cannot be known,
Most go away disappointed.

*****

I tell you:
You must open the doors.
You must pull back
The shutters.
How else can light enter into
A darkened house?

*****

Why fight with
External foes?
Your neighbors are
The very least of
Your problems.

*****

This is Wu Hsin's open secret:
The only evil is inattention.
It is the father of stupidity and
The grandfather of the twins,
Suffering and sorrow.

It is not possible to hurt another
Once one understands that
All anothers are inside oneself and
Emerge from there.

*****

Knowledge will take you
To the goal.
But, not knowledge
Of things.
Knowledge of things will
Distance you from the goal.
Wu Hsin tells you to
Call off your search.

*****

Followers of the sun
Never know darkness.

*****

The Mystery is not reached with words.
Nor can the mind reach It.
Unseen,
Unheard,
It cannot be taught.
What remains is the experiencing
Without an experiencer.

*****

The man of contentment
Seeks nothing that
He doesn't have and
Understands that
Whatever he has
Isn't his to own.

To live and to die
Is natural.
To be afraid
To live and to die is not.

*****

If man spent as much
Time and energy
Demolishing his prison
As was spent in building it,
All would be free.

*****

You are not the main character
In the play.
You are one of many characters.
Each has a role to play.
This realization is
The first step toward
The unity that is, always was and
Always will be.

*****

So many things you could
Give up and
Still not achieve clarity.
Instead,
Simply give up your notions
Of I, me and mine and
Allow stillness to carry you forward.

Forms through which action occurs,
Be it plant, insect, tiger or human
Behave according to their nature.
Understand Nature and
Understand all.

*****

The fundamental question is:
Do you have awareness or
Does Awareness have you?

*****

The world cannot improve until
The peoples of the world improve.
The peoples of the world cannot improve until
The person improves.
The person cannot improve until
All self interest is removed.

*****

The particular and the universal are not separate.
They are merely two aspects of
The indivisible;
One viewed from within,
The other from without.

*****

The desire for understanding
Arises from misunderstanding.
The way out is through
Questioning and examining the habitual.

The animating presence is
The building block upon which
You have been erected.
Even after you have been torn down,
The building block remains.
Centering your attention there is
The direct means to gain
Primordial insight.

*****

What-Is or
You may call it the Truth,
Must be apperceived.
Once one attempts to express it,
It becomes a concept and
Food for discussion.
Then the Truth is lost.
Seekers of Truth must ask:
What distinguishing marks will
Allow one to recognize it?

*****

What does the orange tree
Have to do
To grow oranges?
What does the sky
Have to do
To be blue?
What do you
Have to do
To be?

Wu Hsin takes many
To the river, but
Crosses it for none.

*****

Unhappiness comes to man
Through two doorways
The first doorway is named
Not getting what you want.
The name of the second doorway is
Getting what you want.
Either takes you there;
The former faster
Than the latter.
The former teaches
The futility of willfulness.
The latter teaches the foolishness
Of believing that
Satisfaction and happiness are the same.

*****

When is there to live
Other than now?
How is there to live
Other than now?
Why is there to live
Other than now?
Where is there to live
Other than now?

Desire is presupposed on the belief that
The desired will convey
Some lasting benefit
To the one who desires.
When this is apperceived to be false,
The running after
Persons or things ends and
Impartiality to all that comes and goes
Takes root.

*****

Underneath is the support.
It is the water
To the boat, and
The sky
To the cloud.
The known is supported by
The unknown which, in turn, is
Held by the Unknowable.
Ignoring this is
The folly of men.

*****

Everything moves toward
Its own destruction.
The flame is lit.
The flame is extinguished.
What is between the two is
Labeled time.

Do not confuse
Emptying the pot with
Shattering the pot.
A pot that is emptied
Can be refilled whereas
A shattered pot ceases to be.

*****

It is only when
The very idea of changing is seen
As false that
One can perceive the changeless.

*****

The body is a borrowed thing.
One uses it for a time; then
It must be returned to
That from which it was borrowed.

There is nothing
For me to tell you
That will make a difference.
There is nothing Wu Hsin can say
That will bring about
Your awakening.
The sound of my own voice
Holds no appeal for me.
Nor should you
Be enamored with it.
Ask Wu Hsin to be quiet
This has much more value.
 A viable strategy is to bring about
The end of the questioner.
When there is no questioner,
Then there is no one
Being questioned and
There are no questions.
Within this space
All can be revealed
Most easily.

*****

There is a birth,
A life, and then
A death.
Throughout this cycle of
From the Source - To the Source,
The Source remains ever as it was.
To know the Source is to
Transcend the cycle.

This game being played is
A subtle one;
It begins with the mind
Taking What-Is and
Parsing it into
Millions of pieces.
The balance of the game,
The balance of life, is
Spent trying to
Put it back together.

*****

Clear seeing is elusive
Like trying to capture water
With a net.
The particular net employed is
The belief in the power of
The thinking mind.
For as long as this mind is worshipped,
Clear sight is not to be obtained.
It is little wonder that
The dog chasing its tail
Becomes dizzy.

*****

You are not satisfied
With the answers
Given by others.
So you come to Wu Hsin.
But what you really seek
Are not answers
But confirmation
Of what you think
You already know.
If you were to admit
That you know nothing,
Then I will most gladly answer.

Essence is the size of the sky.
It holds the body and
The mind as if they were
Rose petals in its hands.

*****

The meditation of suffering is
The meditation of:
I am this body
I am this story
I am these thoughts and
I am these emotions.
The meditation of freedom is
The meditation that lacks
A meditator.

*****

All activity to hold on to
That which is
Inherently impermanent is futile and is
The prerequisite for unhappiness.
Releasing all attachment to
The impermanent
Brings with it the revelation of
The face of
The Permanent and is
The harbinger of peace.

Thinking is so tiresome,
Requiring so much energy
Solely for the purpose
Of reinforcing the notion
Of a thinker.
What a waste!
Stop thinking and
Merely watch
Everything being done
Without your interference.

*****

The marriage of
Full consciousness with
Life
Is the most beautiful union
This world has ever known.

*****

You don't know what is good.
You only know
What is good for you.
Tomorrow, that might change.
Then, good will become bad and
You will claim to know it.
All this, however, is relative.
What is good for you
Might be bad for me.
What is good for you today,
Might be bad for you tomorrow.
Wouldn't it be better
To leave the judging
To the fools?

Do not use
Wu Hsin's words
As a platform for
Launching new concepts.
Instead, listen deeply,
Apperceive and then
Forget.
Do not store the words away.
Let them penetrate you,
As would an arrow.

*****

The arrival of what is absent is
Preconditioned on
The departure of
What is present.
So long as
The inn is full
No rooms are available.

*****

I will not tell you
What it looks like
Because then
You will assume that
You know
What you are looking for.
You cannot know it
You can only
Be it and
This being is without cause.
So what is left
For you to do?

Whatever is embraced,
Whatever is clung to, will leave.
Why, then, empower it
By making it important?

*****

When river water is
Placed in a jar
Does its quality change?
The container is irrelevant.
The attention must remain upon
What is of essence.

*****

To fixate on what is not,
The past, the future,
The way things ought to be,
Inherently creates struggle with What-Is.
See this and step out of it.

*****

What is natural
Requires no study or practice for mastery.
Does one study how to sleep?
To reach what is natural
Merely remove what is not natural.

One must either be content with
One's individual accomplishments or
One must break free from
The notion of individuality.

*****

Why do you offer
Such resistance to life?
Has not Wu Hsin told you
That resistance
Only extends and intensifies
Your pain and discomfort.
There is a secret word
Which, when used
With sincerity,
Aligns you with all of life.
That word is
Yes.

*****

Hope requires the future,
Faith dips into the past,
Trust that all is as it should be
In the present moment.

*****

Look deeply inside yourself and
Try to find yourself.
The ensuing failure is
The true finding.

Do not speak to Wu Hsin of
Your godhead experiences.
All experience is dualistic,
Requiring a subject and an object.
Is your godhead an object
To be experienced?

*****

What could be more meaningless
Than to say that
What you are looking at
Is the one who is looking?
However, nothing is closer to the
Primordial way of things than this.
Do you wonder, then,
Why Wu Hsin is laughing?

*****

The antagonism toward the world,
Toward people,
Places and
Things,
Is the impediment
To the realization
Of the peace that
Underlies it all.
Every No keeps peace
An arm's length away.

How many of your questions
Have been answered,
But still
You don't have the answer?
Is it possible that
The answer isn't
Found in more questions?
Is it possible that
The answer isn't
Found in more concepts,
More thoughts?
Is it possible that
The answer is
Revealed in their very absence?

*****

The number of forms
Within this manifestation is
Without limit.
Focusing the attention on
This limitlessness,
It is easy to become lost.
The way back is
The way out.
Return the attention to
That from which
The limitlessness arose.

*****

For the world to change is
Preconditioned on
The acceptance of What-Is.
Once accepted, there is no need
For the world to change.

How glorious is
The purposeless life.
Events occur in
Their natural course and
One need not do anything or
Be anything in particular.
Can there be
A greater freedom than this?

$$*****$$

Chasing after more and more is futile.
It is only less and less that lastingly satisfies.

$$*****$$

In an instant,
There is awakening and
The world arrives,
Unbeckoned.
In a short time,
It recedes and is
Forgotten until
Its next arising.
Understanding the stage on which
This play is performed is
The way out of it.

$$*****$$

Silence is the bridge between
The Formless and
The world of form.

How can light find darkness?
Darkness is merely
The absence of light.
How can one find one's source?
One's source is revealed in
The absence of one's self.

*****

Beyond what?
Beyond where?
Beyond when?
Beyond whom?
This beyond
Is not outside yourself,
But is the vast,
Limitless expanse
Within.
It is not knowable
Nor does it reside
Within the space of the known.
Stop running toward
Positive states.
Stop running from
Negative states.
Stop.
Take whatever comes
As it comes;
Without judgment,
Without embellishment.
Then, watch it pass until
Whatever is to be
Next appears.

The greatest crime is
The overlooking of
Who you really are
In favor of
The story of
Who you think you are.
This preoccupation with
Your personal drama is
The cloud that masks
The sun.

*****

I am sorry
To disappoint you.
But Wu Hsin has no teaching
For you.
No method,
No way,
No system.
Simply be as you are and
All will be right.

*****

Turning the attention
Toward the unfamiliar and
Away from the familiar is a
Prerequisite to the arrival at
True understanding.

Do not accept
Any of the words of Wu Hsin
As the truth.
Investigate for yourself.
This willingness to investigate,
To deeply inquire into
My words, into
Your assumptions, is
The front door to
The house of illumination.

*****

Your hope
For the future is that it will
Bring salvation,
A completion or
A satisfactory conclusion to
Your unsatisfactory past and
The unsatisfactory present.
Wu Hsin tells you that
You are mistaken.

*****

It has taken considerable time
For your illusions
To be built up.
Yet, it takes no time at all
To dissolve them,
To replace them
With simplicity in, and
Acceptance of,
Life.

When a water bubble
On the ocean bursts,
It returns to the ocean.
This is death;
All deaths.
Your death and my death.
Returning to the Source,
What is there to fear?

*****

Expectation is the grandfather of
Disappointment.
The world can never
Own a man
Who wants nothing.

*****

So many aspirants
Seeking understanding from
Magicians,
Meditators,
Representatives of hearsay,
Intellectuals and
World renouncers.
Who amongst these can reveal
The shadow of the Formless?

The body is charged with
Life Force Energy and
Sustained by food.
Where is the role of an individual in this?
It progresses through life
Reacting to people, places and events
In a manner
Specific to its nature.
Where is the role of any individual
In determining this?
Wu Hsin wants to know:
What causes the belief that
You are an individual?

*****

When a gale blows from the east,
Walk to the west.
When a gale blows from the west,
Walk to the east.
Acceptance of the hard and the soft is
The foundation of trust that
All is right.

*****

The adversarial relationship
With life is the prison.
Acceptance of life as it comes,
Day by day,
Moment by moment, is
The key to the lock on the door.

Maturity evolves upon
The realization that
Your numerous strategies
For escaping
Have failed you.
Maturity brings with it
The dawn of understanding of
What it is you are trying
To escape from.
Maturity prompts the examination of
Whether you are really imprisoned at all.

*****

Make no effort to meditate
Make no effort to not meditate
Make no effort to make no effort
Being is not something
One does
Being is what
One is.

*****

Don't come here so that Wu Hsin may
Prescribe a path for you.
Choose the path
Of your inclination,
Regardless of appearances
Or opinion.
All paths meet
At the One Path which goes beyond
All paths.

The necessity to delineate
Right from wrong,
Truth from not-truth,
Is itself the impediment.
The truths of men are finite,
With many nuances.
Primordial Truth
Has infinite expressions
While removing all need
For interpretation.

*****

Prior to the realities of man,
There is an Ultimate Reality.
Many have sought to speak
Its language, but
In the end,
They became ruled
By dogma and ritual.

*****

Every form reflects It,
Yet, It cannot be seen
By the eyes.
In silence,
A subtle, inner eye opens,
That sees the Real
Underlying all appearances.

When names and forms
Are put away,
When all judgment ceases,
What remains is called
The True.
It appears like a mirror
In which the Infinite
Is reflected.
It looks back at each
Who gaze upon It.

*****

Do not allow
Your progress in understanding
To become a concept.
See it as a ladder,
Reaching into the Infinite.
Ladders are not for discussion,
They are for climbing.
It will help you to
Climb to the place
That contains your world,
Yet is beyond it.

*****

Lu Pao had many preoccupations.
Some were large and
Others were small.
When his clothes caught on fire,
None mattered any longer.

A bone with no meat is better
Than no bone at all
To a beggar.
The words of Wu Hsin are
All meat and no bone.
Who is hungry for this?

*****

All necessary work is accomplished
Without actively thinking.
That which moves Wu Hsin
Provides all his words.
Thoughtless,
Wu Hsin cannot be wrong.

*****

Do not divide
Do not label or categorize.
Rather than seeing the many
Within the One,
See the One
Inherent in the many.

*****

If one focuses exclusively on
Dissatisfaction,
The cause of dissatisfaction and
The end of dissatisfaction,
Everything resolves itself in ease.
Don't pretend to be
What you are not;
Don't refuse to be
What you are.

If one saw oneself as
The entire world,
One could do no harm.
Why see oneself as only
Hands,
Feet,
Torso,
Thoughts and feelings?
This is a falsehood.

*****

Every effort
Births more effort.
What has been built
Must be maintained.
What was acquired
Must be protected against loss.

*****

Seeing clearly is
Not mistaking imagination
For reality.
A life seen clearly is
A life without conflict.

All presence, that is,
You,
Me,
It,
Occurs against the background of
Total Absence.
At the end of you,
Me,
It,
Total Absence remains unchanged.

*****

What is pristine knowledge
Other than
The knowledge that
Worldly knowledge isn't worth
A pile of straw.
Admittedly, worldly knowledge can
Take you through the world, but
It can take you neither
Beyond it nor
Before it.

*****

Wu Hsin's motivation is
Easy to understand.
It is the same as
The bird's motivation
To sing.

In the instant of action,
There is no actor.
It is only afterward that
The ego,
This false identity,
Appropriates the action as mine.

*****

When the mind is seen as
Continually kidnapped by thoughts,
The first step toward freedom
Has been taken.
Now, cease listening to
What is being heard.
Instead, listen to
What is listening.

*****

Relinquish the fixation
On beginnings and endings,
On past and future.
All that matters is
This-Now-Here.
Once lost,
It cannot be recovered.

Four questions:
How many more failed strategies
Will you undertake
To gain what you want?
What do you want?
What will getting what you want
Give you?
Who wants to know this?

*****

Everything comes and goes.
That which gave them birth,
Sustained them,
And called them back
Goes by many names.
Wu Hsin prefers Being
Among the list.

*****

Beginning and end
Are not two,
But equal aspects
Of one.
The fruit contains
The seed
Which contains the fruit.

*****

The greatest wealth is contentment.
The greatest happiness is
Freedom from opinions.
The greatest peace is attained
Through the abandonment of desires.

If one desires clear sight
One cannot place one's trust in reflections.
The way in is
The only way out.

*****

The room was filled with
Hundreds of his devotees
When Chow Ling asked,
"Why are you worshipping the teapot
Instead of drinking the tea?"

*****

Many there are
Who come to Wu Hsin for help
With their search.
Wu Hsin says he cannot help;
The search must fail, because
All searching is for some thing and
This Sought is no thing.
If it is not an object,
How may it be found?

*****

From the point of view of
The person
Problems never cease.
From the point of view of
The Totality
Problems never arise.
Perfection is disturbed by
The arrival of judgment.

Just sitting;
Without a goal,
Without a schedule,
Without an intention,
Without form and
Without deliberateness.
The seed opens into the fruit.
Just sitting.

*****

There are some who
Retire to the forests and mountaintops
To avoid involvement with
The world.
Yet, the inner involvement continues.
Every thought
Cries out for involvement.
This is the involvement from which
Retirement is to be sought.

*****

To conquer the large,
Begin with the small.
To change your world,
Begin by changing yourself.
What needs to be changed?
Only the point of view.

*****

The calligrapher begins with
White parchment;
Nothingness.
From there,
All emergence is possible.

In the presence of fuel,
The oil lamp generates flame.
When the fuel is exhausted,
The flame is extinguished.
The lamp remains,
Ever as it was.

*****

The experience of one's birth is not personal.
Therefore, it is not remembered.
Lao Yin lost his memory and
Could not speak
Concerning his personality.

*****

There is no scripture
That can take you
Beyond the world.
Nor is any meditation or
Ritual the modality.
Wu Hsin counsels that
You stop deceiving yourself.

*****

Man is a part
Of the Largeness
Called Nature.
One part in an infinity of parts.
None higher,
None lower.
Each has value and
Fulfills its purpose.
Do not interfere.

You are a microcosm
Of the cosmos.
Your body is comprised of
All the elements
Of the world.
The cosmos has donated itself
To make you.
The day will come
When she will request a refund.
Grant it smilingly.

*****

Do not mistake birth
For beginning.
Likewise,
Death is not
An ending.
Prior to birth is
Existence without limit.
This is the quality
That is masked
By incarnation.
Remove the mask and
Remove the bindings.

*****

Emergence is
The realization of
Potentiality.
Things appear,
Stay and ultimately depart.

Grace appears
In the world
Like a giant cloud
Pouring refreshment
On the parched and
On the thirsty.
The closed ones
Fail to partake
Fail to benefit
Because they are
Otherwise engaged.

*****

Will adding copper to gold
Improve it?
What is inherent in each
Needs no improvement.
What is not inherent is not
Worthy of attention.

*****

What comes
Will go.
Only the permanent is beyond
Coming and going.
How much time is left,
One minute or fifty years?
Why squander it on
The transient?

*****

Liberation does not occur
To any thing in the outer.
It is an inner experience of
Freedom from attachments to the outer.
The saint in prison is free,
The emperor is bound.

Save your time.
Do not come to Wu Hsin.
What you seek
Is below;
It is above.
It is behind you and
In front of you.
To the north,
South,
East and
West.

*****

Follow Wu Hsin,
If you can.
I follow the path
Left behind by birds
In flight;
The trails of fish.
And I answer to no one.
How can leaves grow
On a tree with
No branches?

*****

Believing oneself to be
The author of one's life is
No different than being
The piglet of a barren sow.

Desirousness is
A bottomless well
The only route
To its bottom is
Through desirelessness
When your feet touch
Solid ground
Then you are free.

*****

Being aware of
The sound of the bell
Does not mean that
The bell belongs to you.
Likewise, being aware of thoughts
Does not mean that
The thoughts belong to you.

*****

The shadow cannot exist
Without the substance, but
The shadow is not
The substance.
How can the world exist for you
If you are not present
To perceive it?

*****

Creation stories are for children.
The world is created in
Every new moment.
Stand aside and simply marvel.

Singular wholeness is always the same.
It is unchanging.
That which changes may appear on it.
It is unchanging.

*****

Where is the observed
In the absence of
The observer?
If the observed object requires
A subjective observer
Is not this subjective observer
Also an object?
Where, then, is
The true Subject?
Since the true Subject
Is not an object
The true Subject
Cannot be found and
The notion of where
Loses all meaning.

*****

This mystery fulfills all its functions unceasingly
Even though it appears to be
Silent and unmoving.
It is the field upon which
The knower and that which is known meet.

Wu Hsin is not different from you
Except that he owns fewer things,
Owns fewer opinions,
Owns fewer concepts,
Owns fewer thoughts.

*****

Renewal requires destruction.
The old must be torn down before
The new can be erected.

*****

Wu Hsin is so full that
Nothing can be added.
Wu Hsin is so empty that
Nothing can be removed.
The outer world of perceptions,
The inner world of thoughts,
Wu Hsin is neither yet
The knower of both.

*****

Nothing succeeds like failure.
Failure is a natural
Call for attention,
Like pain.
To pay attention is to
Step out of your trance.

*****

To free the chick,
The shell must be broken.
To free what is inside
One must shatter
What is outside.

The key to understanding is
The dissolution of
The barriers between
Subject and object,
Knower and known and
Seer and seen.
In this condition,
One cannot locate
The markers of separation.

*****

What is known is familiar
Yet unsatisfying.
What is unknown is feared
Yet desired
Life thrives in risks and
Dies in stasis.
Live.

*****

The Master is not the goal
Fixation on the Master
Impedes reaching the goal
Releasing the Master
Releasing all ideations
About the goal
Takes one a long way
Toward the goal.

*****

To destroy the ego
One must first find it.

The bell rings then
The sound ends.
Hearing awaits.
The fruit is sweet,
Now the taste is gone.
Tasting remains.
Believing oneself to be
What comes and goes is
High folly.

*****

Men are so entranced by
The tree
That they have forgotten
The seed,
The source of the tree.
Forgetting the source is what
Keeps men from
The source.

*****

How much time does it take
To apperceive conditions as they are?
It takes much less time than
You have and
Much less time than
You're willing to allocate.
By now, it could be completed
If only you could relinquish
Your stranglehold on appearances.

When there is hunger and
Food is provided,
Does one say that the mouth has
Compassion for the stomach?
When there are no others
There is no compassion.

*****

What is a name?
What is a form?
Are they not the symbols
Of someone who
Regards himself as separate?
The name….
Is it not merely
The name of an ego?
But the Nameless has no name.
Wu Hsin asks:
"Where does one end
And the other begin?"

*****

The wheel of becoming
Spins unceasingly.
Becoming this,
Becoming that………….
When one steps off of the wheel,
What has always been,
What need never become, is illuminated.

All the strategies you use
To protect yourself are actually
The chains that
Keep you bound.
To be free of the world
You must be free of yourself.
The fear that is experienced
When you consider
What must be done is merely
These strategies fighting
For their survival.
Ignore what you hear
Ignore what you may tell yourself and
Trust that which
Wu Hsin tells you is
The way out.

*****

This morning
I take my pen in hand
To write
But who or what
Is it that writes?
Is it the pen?
Is it Wu Hsin?
Is it both
Or neither?
Wu Hsin moves the pen
But what is it
That moves Wu Hsin?

*****

The world changes profoundly
When demands on it cease.
The real world and one's imagined world
Share little.

Ridding oneself of ignorance is
Worth more than the acquisition of knowledge.
With memory gone
The past is gone
Relinquishing hopes and fears
The future is gone.
The present is upon you.
In every moment.
You are free.

*****

My friends come to me
And speak of acquiring merit
Through good deeds
Wu Hsin asks "Why?"
They tell me
It is the way to Heaven.
Yet when Wu Hsin asks
"What is it that goes to Heaven?"
All fall silent.

*****

What needs to be revealed
Reveals itself by itself.
No coaxing, no persuasion,
No effort at all is required.
It shines by itself and
Needs no illumination from the outside.

*****

No mountain has only one side.
At times, it is sunny on one side and
Raining on the other.
The side that has seen the sun
Will experience the rain.

A comfortable bed does not
Lessen the discomfort of
A nightmare.
This is only achieved by
Waking up from the nightmare.

*****

Put the time, attention and energy
That you use trying to get
What you think you want
To better use.
Getting what you thought you wanted
Has never brought you
Lasting happiness.
Instead, use the time, attention and energy to
Realize the fullness that is
Ever present and
All around you.

*****

Who dies
When the body dies?
What dies?
In this inquiry,
The sun burns away the fog and
The mists lift.

*****

To have no thought and
To make no effort is
The first step toward Understanding.
The second step is
To go nowhere and
To do nothing.
Upon completion of these,
Resting for a while is advised.

Each being is a moment in time
With a name and
A form and
A script
To be performed
In this play called
Life.
None chose the name
Nor the form
Nor the script
Yet each believes himself to be
The master of his destiny.
Once their sight clears,
They, too, will laugh.

*****

Awakening occurs
Not when there is no more
To be added
But instead,
When there is no more
To be taken away.

*****

I am a shadow,
A reflection mistaken for its image,
An echo mistaken for its voice,
A ghost mistaken for its substance.
My true substance
Is found in
Every Moment
Of Being
Present
Now.

Two men from the province of Yi,
Debating the predominance of the will over destiny,
Or vice versa,
They are the source
Of many laughs
For Wu Hsin
Those who have real knowledge,
Not concepts
Or the knowledge of things
Are free
From both free will
And destiny.
They are lions
Who follow no path
But their own.

*****

What could be simpler to understand?
Whoever thinks as, or on behalf of,
An entity
Which he thinks he is,
Who works on this himself
Through prayer,
Fasting,
Meditation,
Ritual or
Good works
Has not yet begun to understand
What it is all about.

Moving the eyes from
The front of the face to
Behind the head
Allows for the clear perception that
One is not separate from manifestation,
But rather a part of it.
The space that fills the small pot is
The same as the space
That fills the large pot.

*****

A ripple appeared on the lake in Guangzhou.
Most who saw it
Became interested in the ripple and
Forgot about the lake.
The world has many distractions,
Its background has none.

*****

Over the parched earth,
Rain clouds appear.
Yet, one cannot
Make it rain.
The ingredient that must be added is
Waiting.
To wait in the face of urgency
Is to understand that
All is as it is intended.

One's god cannot be reached
Through a beggar's bowl.
Asking for the fulfillment of wants,
For the world's acquiescence
To one's will,
Insults the very deity
That is prayed to
By revealing that
Trust in this god is absent.

*****

Illusion holds enormous power
Until its reality is investigated
The greatest illusion is that
There is a line
Of demarcation separating
Me and you.

*****

Flirting with time is
A losing game.
In the end,
Time eats everything except
The timeless.

Man lives through his fictions.
He acts as if
He will not die.
He acts as if
There are gods that
Reward and punish.
He acts as if
He controls his life,
Controls his destiny.
It need not be otherwise;
The next moment will
Take care of itself.
Substance is immanent in
Every shadow.
This is the gate without a gate that
One must pass through
To attain understanding.

*****

Are you willing to risk
Everything, to be
Totally and utterly exposed?
Are you willing to see
How you defraud.
Demean and trivialize
The totality of your being
By relegating it to
This psychosomatic device
Called you?
Or would you rather
Be fishing?
The ability to discriminate
Between what appears to be and
What-Is is
The mark of the wise.
They reside at the hub
Of the wheel
While others
Revolve around the rim.

Involvement is the
Father of happiness and the
Mother of sorrow.
In the absence of involvement,
The pendulum stops swinging and
Peace and balance prevail.

*****

Being clean is
Its own reward.
It is the same with
Being free from
That which is false.

*****

As long as you are,
A doer,
Whether doing or not doing,
Thinking or not thinking,
Meditating or not meditating
This you is
No closer to home
Than it was
On the day
It left home.

*****

Your mind's problems are not
Your problems.
Why get involved?
Seeing the false as false is enough.

Wu Hsin is like white paper
Before it is touched
By the pen.
Once the strokes are put down,
The white paper is ignored.

*****

Can we agree that
Madness is little more than
The searching outside for what
Can only be found within?
To change the face in the mirror,
One doesn't change the mirror.

*****

Seeing requires two components:
The seer and
That which is seen.
In the absence of a seer,
Nothing is seen.
When there is nothing to be seen,
There is no seer.
As the seer and the seen are
Interdependent,
So is all of this play called
Life.

*****

The recognition of what one is not
Goes a long way toward illuminating
What one is.

What comes and goes is
Merely an appearance.
That which perceives all
Comings and goings is
The only substance.
Drinking this elixir,
Life is recognized to be eternal.

*****

Staying sacred isn't difficult.
Its sole requirement is
The removal of one's lips
From the mouth of the profane.
Then sacredness blossoms like
Flowers in the Spring.

*****

The relinquishing of all searching
Allows the immobility to arise
That reveals
That there is no becoming;
All already is.

*****

The world may be divided into
Three parts:
The known,
The unknown and
The Unknowable.
It is to the last that
One must go
So that you may receive
What you are after.

The loss of habitual certainties is
The gain of clear vision.
The common man looks at things,
Uncommon man sees through them.

*****

Upon the arrival of
The great death,
All concerns for
The lesser death
Disappear.
Somebody becomes
No body in particular and
Life goes on without fear.

*****

Wu Hsin does not possess
The pass key to heaven nor
The escape route from hell.
Both are available
On this earth and are chosen
In every moment.

*****

Everything can be seen in daylight,
Except daylight.

*****

The play is
An illusion;
The stage is not.
In the absence of
A distinct seer and
A distinct seen
All that remains is
The seeing.

Every being is
An object
To every other being
Which considers itself to be
The subjective.
This misunderstanding explains
The reason men believe
They can act in a manner
That is counter to what is natural.
But this is only a belief and
Wu Hsin tells you that
Most of what you believe is wrong.

*****

The newborn fish does not
Learn to swim.
It swims.
The swimming arises from
The natural state of things.
Abiding in what is natural,
One cannot make mistakes.

*****

A common error is to believe that
The Eternal will reveal Itself to you
On your terms, in your time and
In your way.
Throw away all notions and
Simply be willing
To see.

Doing or not doing;
Pick either,
Only do not attach value to
The outcome of either.
In this manner,
The flow of peace
Remains uninterrupted.

*****

If Wu Hsin's words
Create a resonance, then
He is called a wise man.
If they do not,
He is dismissed as
A bag of feces.
The words are the same,
The hearer is not.

*****

With the willingness to bear
Whatever comes,
Comes the end of
The need of
Any and all strategies and
Safety is recognized as
The illusion that it is.

It is not possible to love the world
Without loving oneself first.
Is one not
Part of the world rather than
Apart from it?
Love the smaller first,
Then the greater.
In so doing, the space between
Oneself and the world disappears;
One becomes the world.

*****

Mo Hua,
The wise old man from Li Jiang.
Daily rode in his horse-drawn cart.
Although it took him
Wherever he wanted to go,
He never mistook
His cart for himself.

*****

When the specialness is relinquished,
All is well and natural.
When the gold necklace is melted down,
Is it not still gold?

*****

Names and forms,
The content of perception,
Comprise the world.
The world exists
Because one exists.
But one is not the world,
Only its knower.
The proof is that
The arising of the knower
Precedes the arising of the world.

The same power that is
Plowing the fields is
Cutting the vegetables and
Moving the wind.
It resides in every thing to
The special benefit of none.

*****

Place your ear into the
Heart of Wu Hsin.
Hear the words
Before they are spoken.
Absorb them directly by
Bypassing the mind.
This is the most direct means.

*****

The notion that human life
Has greater value
Than any other form of life is
The greatest demonstration of arrogance.

*****

The harder the wood,
The hotter the flame.
The stronger the personality,
The brighter the light generated
Upon its demise.

The arising of any thought,
Feeling or emotion, is
Independent of the person.
It is only when involvement
By a person occurs, that
The thought, feeling, or emotion
Becomes personal.

*****

When naturalness is lost
Ideations and concepts rush in to
Fill the void.
Wholeness is seemingly lost when
The world is viewed with self interest.

*****

Darkness cannot reveal
The color of a flower.

*****

For how long
Have you been seeking unity
With your particular god?
Why has it eluded you?
Wu Hsin suggests that you cease
Searching for this jewel.
The necklace has,
All the time,
Been around your neck.

*****

Your only asset is
The presence of awareness.
With it, you are everything,
Without it,
What are you?

Do not plan to make changes.
If change is required,
It will arrive
In its own time.
Wait and watch.

*****

Every scene is a preparation
For the subsequent scene.
The sum of the scenes is
Life.

*****

Is pain the interval
Between two pleasurable experiences or
Is pleasure the interval
Between two painful experiences?
The absence of both,
The absence of thought,
This interval is
Evenness and tranquility.

*****

Man is solely an intermediary
Standing between What-Is and
Its designed outcome.
Instruments produce actions
But take no credit for results.

*****

If you want to know the truth
You must be able to recognize falsehood.
Once the false is removed,
The true stands illuminated.

You see before you
This body called Wu Hsin.
But Wu Hsin is not the body.
Wu Hsin is
The seeing,
The hearing,
The perceiving,
The smelling and
The tasting of all that is
Seen, Heard,
Perceived,
Smelled and tasted.
The attention never goes to stillness;
It always goes toward movement.
The stillness,
That which is prior to movement, is
Therefore missed.
Pay attention and
See things as they really are.
What other discipline is required?

*****

-

Personal freedom is
Nothing more than
Freedom from the personal.
As such, personal freedom is
Not available to any body.

*****

The easiest method to remove
The ongoing condition of vigilance is to
Remove the me whom
The vigilance protects.
Then, vigilance dissolves.

Devotion to any teacher, any sage,
Perpetuates the illusion of
Division and separation.
That which animates the teacher
Animates all.
Direct one's devotion to That.

*****

The wise man does not
Need the people's prayers.
The wise man is
The answer to
The people's prayers.

*****

When the tendency to
Manipulate and control
Every experience ceases,
A new world arises,
Filled with a balance and a peace
Previously unexperienced.

Ascetics are everywhere.
They renounce shelter,
Work,
Fine clothing,
Speech and
Lifestyle.
But they are self deluded.
True renunciates renounce concepts,
Ideas,
Opinions,
Judgments,
Hopes,
Past and
Future.
Show Wu Hsin a single one of these.

*****

Happiness comes, happiness goes.
Stop chasing it.
Sorrow comes, sorrow goes.
Stop running from it.
Relax into what doesn't come and go,
What is present in every moment,
In every here and now.

*****

How can a man be free
Who is attached to so many things?

There are many who practice to develop
Wisdom,
Generosity,
Patience and
Discipline.
In this fashion,
These are the products of the practice.
Wu Hsin notes that with
Clear understanding,
All these arise as
By-products while
No practice is required.

*****

One seeking transcendent wisdom
Embarks on a journey where
The mind cannot go.
It is only in the
Absence of preconceptions that
What-Is can be revealed.

*****

There can be no observer
In the absence of
An observed object.
The two comprise
One whole.
Fold oneself
Into oneself and
Simply be
The subjective witness of
One's objective expression.

All aspiration is self deception.
It is preconditioned on
The arrival of tomorrow.
What can arrive tomorrow
Can likewise be had in
This moment if
The view is right.

*****

The stream of mind is
A continuous flow.
To believe that one can
Permanently stop it is like
Believing in one's success at
Burying one's shadow.
Once this is realized,
It, too, is accepted.

*****

When the path narrows.
Stand aside to allow
Those rushing forward
To pass you by.
The goal is not to arrive,
The goal is to
Fully experience the journey.

*****

The mind,
The body and
The world are not separate.
They arise together,
They set together.
Upon apperceiving this,
Methods are seen as useless.

Everything arises from
A single source which
Resides in the space between.
It can only be reached
Through removal and negation.
Take away this thought,
Take away that object and
What remains is
What-Is.

*****

Inside a cloud,
The vision is limited.
Outside the cloud,
The cloud is seen.
Other clouds are seen.
The sun is seen.
The sky is seen and
The moon and the stars.
This is Wu Hsin's invitation:
Step out of the cloud.

*****

All goals,
All getting,
Serve to only strengthen the ego.
The recognition
That there is nothing
To be gained or attained,
That everything is already
Here and now, is wisdom.

Like water is shaped by its container,
Man is shaped by
The essences of the parents and
The experiences of life.
Controlling neither,
One is what one is.

*****

Never mind the mind.
It is like pouring droplets of water into
A hot frying pan.

*****

When one is struck by awe or wonder,
There is no line of separation between
The knower and the known.
In this space, the world and
Every act in it is spontaneous.

*****

Real happiness is causeless.
Happiness that is caused is not real;
It is transient.
Believing that the transient
Can take one to
The intransient is
Self deception.

*****

All musts are false.
No must can be spontaneous and
Only that which is spontaneous is
Real.

The creation of distinctions
Births the cycle of pleasure and pain.
When everything is
Accepted with equanimity,
Calm is established.

*****

Wu Hsin plants a seed
In the ground and waits for
The right season to arrive when
It will sprout and
Grow and
Become a mighty tree.

*****

Looking through colored glass
Colors what you see.
What keeps you from clearly seeing
What is real is the colored glass of
The mind.
Its preferences,
Its dramas and,
Its need to evaluate are
Keeping you from that
Which you believed
Wu Hsin could provide.

*****

All conflict
Between friends, lovers,
Family or states
Begins as conflict inside yourself.
Freeing yourself from conflict
Frees the world of conflict.

Words and concepts
Are not to be regarded as
Systems or methods to be adhered to.
They merely facilitate a
Deepening of understanding.
They are a source of stimulation, and
Nothing more.
Adopted as regimen,
They are a hindrance.

*****

How many of the seemingly earnest are
Devoting their energies to
The attainment of liberation
Which, by its most rigorous definition,
Is unattainable?
Is not the egoic striver
The real barrier
Between what one thinks one is and
That which one wishes to become?
How can one become
What one has always been and always will be?
Does sugar suddenly become sweet?

*****

You are not your cart,
Nor are you the horse pulling it.
You are the knower of both and
The identity of neither.

*****

Time can tear down mountains.
Consider what the timeless source of time can do!

Before there is clarity,
Everything is viewed through a keyhole.
After there is clarity,
The door has been removed.

*****

Desire is the urge to be happy.
Desirelessness is the
Fruit of the recognition of
Inherent happiness.

*****

The accumulation of knowledge does not
Lead to omniscience.
Knowing what needs to be known,
For every moment,
In every moment is omniscience.
It begins with
Knowing one's mind.

*****

One who feeds
The wolves of excess is never alone
Nor ever appeased.
By making oneself lower,
One attains the highest.

*****

Long ago,
Wu Hsin used to be somebody.
Now, he is in all things and
All things are in him and
He has become
No body in particular.

Being in the Way, that is,
Alignment with Divine Intention
Means simply not to
Be in the way.

*****

Freedom is not something
One possesses.
Freedom is
That which possesses.

*****

Until one escapes from
The prison of the body,
For every inside, there will be
An outside.

*****

Morality is an illusion;
Who can stop
The movement of the world?
Who can improve upon the sacred?

*****

It is only the empty man
Who understands and embodies
The subtleties of subtraction.
It is he who is intimate with
The Mother of all things.

Life is the oscillation between
Pleasure and pain.
However, pleasure is not happiness.
Pleasure is momentary,
Dependent on circumstances or things.
Happiness depends on nothing.

*****

What further evidence is required
To prove your complete distrust of
Your god
Beyond the fact that
You worry about tomorrow?

*****

So many fear aloneness.
This is the great paradox.
Upon the realization that
There is no other,
Aloneness is understood to be
What is natural.

*****

What follows is
A listing of things
One must do
To attain Oneness:

*****

To make Wu Hsin laugh,
One need merely talk
About one's feeling of disconnection.
Wu Hsin sees the thirsty fish.
Wu Hsin laughs and laughs.

Just as water is serene
When it is free of ripples,
Likewise, the mind is serene
When it is free of thought.
Free of thought:
Free of judgment,
Free of discrimination,
Free of defense
Free of agenda and
Free of strategy.
Free.

*****

Awareness alone exists.
Prior to the arising of things,
Awareness simply is.
Upon the arising,
Awareness is conscious of things.
Things come,
Things go.
Birth, growth, dissolution.
Amidst it all,
Awareness is the Unmovable;
No where to go to,
No where to come from.

*****

Every man is a star in the sky
Appearing,
Moving for a time and then gone.
Each star fulfills its purpose
Without concern for whether
Its movements are right or wrong.

As the long, winding road
Unwinds,
The sense of specialness
Disappears and is replaced by
The apperception of the unity
With every thing.

*****

Only this now-moment is eternal and real.
All else is mind.
Spontaneity is presence in the present.
Where is the place for mind there?

*****

To smell the flowers
Growing amidst the pile of garbage,
One must choose where to place
The attention.
This challenge goes on
In every moment until one can utter
"This too".

*****

Whatever is perceived is transitory.
It came, it will go; it is imperfect.
The One who knows the imperfect is
Perfect.

*****

There is nothing new here.
Wu Hsin puts forth
That which is most ancient.

This life that you speak of,
This life that you tell your friends about,
This life that you are so unhappy with;
Whose life is it?
When mine is seen for the mirage that it is
Then silence fills the void made by its absence.

*****

Everything you think,
Everything you do, is for your self
But who is this self that is
Claimed as yours?
And who is the claimer?
My body,
My thoughts,
My feelings and emotions.
You are not them.
Because they are yours, separate.
Show Wu Hsin you're "my".

*****

The past is only
A memory.
The future is only
A hope.
All there is,
Is this moment.

*****

The deep understanding,
The clear seeing
That there is no liberation
Is itself,
Liberation.

Do not speak to me of the Truth
As if Truth is something to be led around on a rein
Or bottled.
Truth resides in a dimension beyond thought.
Beyond concepts.

*****

The beggar's bowl may be made of
Pure gold, but if
The beggar does not know this, then
He is a pauper.

*****

Unity has no thoughts
Because, in unity
There is no thing to think about.

*****

Wu Hsin cannot help you
Find your god.
Your god is somebody,
My god is no body.
Your god is somewhere,
My god is everywhere.
Your god is something,
My god is no thing, yet
Everything.
How can you expect Wu Hsin to help you?
Wu Hsin cannot separate the flame from
The fire.

Stop demanding that
Life provide happiness.
Happiness is inherent and
Internal to Being.
Looking for happiness in the external
May provide heat, but no light.

*****

The Great Mystery
Cannot be thought through to solution.
In a single flash,
Clear Seeing occurs and
The Mystery is dissolved.

*****

Memory is undependable.
Selective,
Sporadic,
Exaggerating and
Distorting,
It is an unreliable storehouse.
That which is unreliable
Must not be empowered.

*****

As the sugar is completed pervaded
By the sugar cane juices,
This world is pervaded by
The Light.
When the Light shines;
All is seen.

My method has
No method.
You need only to stop.
Stop clinging,
Stop scheming,
Stop praying,
Stop seeking,
Stop analyzing,
Stop all your strategies and lastly,
Stop giving your thoughts
The authority to define
Who you are.
Simply allow what remains to
Reveal Itself.

*****

Wu Hsin will not
Engage you in debate.
Debate is food for
The mind.
My preference is not to
Feed the mind but to
Starve it.

*****

Reject the path
Reject the journey,
Reject the desire to become
Anything in particular.
Reject time itself and
Become enveloped in what remains.

What is realization?
Realization is the understanding
That there is no one to be realized.
Nothing else.

*****

What one was before this,
What one will be after this, is
No different from
What one is now.
Prior to a body,
Prior to a mind,
Prior to a personality,
This is It.

*****

Chasing what is impermanent
Brings joy on the
Day of acquisition and
Sorrow on the day of loss.
Why not chase
What is permanent instead?

*****

Man is not possessed
By a separate self.
He is merely possessed by
His belief in one.

*****

Do not look at me.
I come before you to
Point you to the sun.
Do not look at me.
Look at the sun.

Why do you complain
About the darkness
When there are unlit candles
Beside your bed?
It's really quite simple:
Know what you are not,
Everything that you are not.
What remains is what you are and
Have always been.

*****

Wherever there are others
There is a separate self,
Wherever there are no others
There can be no self,
Wherever there is no self
There are no others,
Because in the absence of self,
One is all others.

*****

The temples and monasteries
Cannot hide you
When you are running away
From yourself.
There is no sanctuary
Other than to dive inward and
Investigate who is running away
From what?

Over the course of your life
Your image of yourself
Keeps changing.
Wu Hsin wants to know
Why you convey
So much power to
Something so undependable?

*****

It is only through
Losing one's mind that
One may come to
One's senses.
All else is like
Trying to smooth water.

*****

What is before birth and
What is after death is
The identical vastness.
A life is only the briefest
Interlude between the two.

*****

Identification is bondage.
Whether it is identification
With a thought
With a feeling
Or with an object
It matters not.
Only identification with the Limitless is
Freedom.

If it may be so called,
My Concept is the
Concept of no concepts,
My Practice is the
Practice of non-practice and,
The Method of meditation is
By non-meditation,
This results in the Mind of no mind,
The Thought of no thought and,
The Action of no action.
In summation,
It is The Presence of the
Absence of volition,
Which is awakening.

*****

Nothingness:
Wanting nothing
Getting nothing
Having nothing
Needing nothing
Doing nothing
Being nothing
Being no thing.
This is Freedom.
This is Fullness.

*****

Life is
Its own purpose.
There is nothing
That needs to be done and
There is no one to do it.

The dissatisfaction with,
The insufficiency of,
This moment is
All that need be transcended.
The door to
This transcendence is to be
Found in acceptance.

*****

Habitual and normal are
Not the same.
Nor are
Different and separate.
Herein, the confusion lies.

*****

The person is a collection of
Habits and memories.
Who is it to whom
The person happens?

*****

In every instant
There is change.
Nothing is constant.
Where can one find
Security in this?
One cannot,
So why use so much energy
Attempting to do so?

No one is humble
There is only
Humility
No one is compassionate
There is only
Compassion
Removing the one
Reveals the One.

*****

Although preparation for change
May be gradual,
All true change is sudden.

*****

Seeing clearly is an impersonal event
Occurring in the absence of
One intending to see clearly.
In fact, it is the one
Intending to see clearly
That is the very impediment to
Seeing clearly.

*****

Wu Hsin would happily
Provide you with a way.
But how does one go
From here to here?

How do you
Describe color
To a man
Blind from birth?
All this talking,
Why?
Let the Stillness
Speak
And all questions are answered.

*****

In an instant,
An entire world is created
When you dream.
The dreamer merely watches,
Having no control over what
The dreamed characters are doing.
Then you awaken.
In an instant,
An entire world is created.

*****

In the moment when
The sight meets
The mirror
There comes an explosion in understanding
That there is no difference
Between the two.

One may teach it to you
Using five thousand words
While another
Teaches it
Using only five.
This should not be
A source of worry.
Your ears will go to
The one they can hear.

*****

The dungeon of individuality is a cold keeper.
Liberation is liberation
From the idea of liberation.
The essence of what
You see before you are
The infinite reflections of
A single lamp.

*****

If the words are heard,
Fully heard, not just
Listened to,
Then the work is over:
You are
What you have always been and
Always will be.
Therefore, what is left
To be done or undone?
And who is to do it?

The central problem is not that
You think too highly
Of yourself
Nor is it that
You think too lowly
Of yourself.
Instead, it is that
You think constantly
Of yourself.

*****

The failure to understand
The Great Mystery
Resides in the inability to perceive
What should be obvious
Due to a conditioned response
That causes the looker
To always be looking in
The wrong direction.

*****

My shadow is real
Because it can be observed;
It is unreal
Because it cannot exist
Independent of me.
I am real
Because I can be observed;
I am unreal
Because I cannot exist
Independent of That
Which supports and preceded me.

To be free of the obsession
With the future,
With the preoccupation of
What to do next, is
Most well regarded by those that
Others label as lazy.
Even if it were so,
It would be
The highest form of laziness.

*****

Wishing for a better past,
A different past,
Is the cornerstone of unhappiness.
Awash in the present,
In every What-Is,
Joy is boundless.

*****

When expectation and wants
Are set aside,
The flow
Of the natural is unimpeded.
Life softens
And ease arises
And one is that much closer to peace.

*****

Roots wither in darkness.
Keeping the root healthy and
Well watered
Will insure that
The fruits are sweet.
Attention should always be
Directed to the root.

There is nothing that Wu Hsin has
That another doesn't have
In equal measure.
As such, what has Wu Hsin
To give anyone,
Other than the awareness of
Our equality?

*****

Becoming has no beginning.
Becoming has no end.
Becoming merely restarts itself
In every instant.
Becoming this or that is
A movement away from it.

*****

The universal is everywhere and
In every thing, yet
It cannot be discerned
With eyes that are personal.

*****

The guises you employ
To protect yourself
From the world
Also deny you
Full access to your heart.
To love fully and completely
Demands the willingness
To be annihilated.

Achieving immortality is easy.
Only set aside
Ownership of body and mind and
Remain rooted in what was there
Before their appearance.

*****

This knowledge came upon me
In a flash:
I sought to remember
What I was before
Thoughts arrived, before
The sense of the body arrived, before
This me was born.
What was revealed was that
I was birthed from Nature,
From the Totality of every thing.
Shackled by time,
Shackled by an identification
Of my own making,
With smallness.
And when I am done, I will
Return there;
The cycle will be complete.

*****

Why are you so afraid of life?
Why do you distrust it so?
Why must you control
Every aspect of
The environment around you?
Why must you defend yourself
Against another's words or actions,
Regardless of how trivial?
Why?

For something to be seen
Or known
Or perceived or cognized,
There must be
A subject and
An object.
That which you seek is
Prior to these.
How will you know it
When you find it?
How can you find it
When it isn't an it?
The notion of I is
A basket into which
So many other notions are thrown.
Upon deep examination,
The basket is revealed to be empty.

*****

Name and form are a unit of time,
Emerging from and returning to
The Timeless.

*****

Birth and death are merely
The beginning and ending of
A series of events.
Stand on the outside,
Observe them but
Don't get involved.
Standing on the high cliff,
The river below can be
Observed and enjoyed without
The observer getting wet.

The promise of the future is
A falsehood.
How many futures have come and gone
While dissatisfaction remains?

*****

Once the great awakening occurs
Whatever ensues afterwards is of no consequence.
Outward changes may occur,
They may not.
Outward signs need not announce
Inner transformation.

*****

What is your life other than
The functioning of
The Totality from
The viewpoint of
The specific?

*****

The very next second
Holds the possibility that
You can disengage from
Your enchantment with
You life story and
You can enter into
The realm of
Complete peace.
Wu Hsin wants to know:
What are you waiting for?

Admittedly, we are all objects
Known to the senses of one another.
Yet, the knower of all objects
Must exist
Prior to all objects.
Therefore, how can the knower
Be known?

*****

Only an object
Can manifest
The effect of a cause
But an object
Cannot know the effect.
The subject
Knows the effect.
Suffering arises
When the supposed subject
Mistakes itself
For the object.
The end of suffering
Is the end
Of objectification
By the supposed subject.

*****

True innocence requires
The willingness to be hurt,
The willingness to be wrong,
The willingness to be awed and
Out of control.
True innocence is
The doorway to
The eternal.

In the beginning,
There were no others.
Then I arrived,
You arrived,
They arrived
And peace departed.

*****

All that happens is
The cause of
All that happens.
Every event requires
The cooperation of
The totality.

*****

All this running
Back and forth
In the name of doing.
What does a rose do
In order to smell
Like a rose?
What does the sky do
So that it may be
The sky?
Wu Hsin says
All doing is inherent in being.
Be.
Wu Hsin is not
The sun.
The sun that knows
No night
Was before Wu Hsin
And is after Wu Hsin
Yet during Wu Hsin.
Who is Wu Hsin, therefore
To speak of nothingness?

Everything you have had
Will be lost.
Everything you have
Will be lost.
Everything you will have
Will likewise be lost.
Why make them important?

*****

Using your mind will not
Take you to Freedom.
How can the mind
Name the Nameless,
Grasp the Formless or
Know that which cannot
Be known?
This tool cannot
Cultivate this field.

*****

The success of Wu Hsin
Rests on one act,
That being,
Keeping myself
Away from myself.
It was not anything I did
It was only
What was done.

*****

The recognition of illusion as illusion
Does not necessarily
End the illusion.
However, it ends the involvement
With the illusion.
This is enough.

In order to achieve Understanding
One's focus need be less on
What one is
And more on
What one is not.
When the clouds
All disappear
The sun is revealed
In its full splendor.

*****

You are dreaming
My child:
Dreaming that you are asleep
Dreaming that you are awake.
All the while
Life is being lived.

*****

What is required
To keep your problems alive?
The answer to this is your
Meditation on your suffering.
Freedom from pain
Freedom from suffering is only
Freedom from my pain
Freedom from my suffering.
True freedom is
Freedom from "my".

The people believe
That the answer to happiness
Lies in having more,
Acquiring more.
Wu Hsin tells you
This is an error.
Having twice as much
Doesn't make one
Twice as happy.
Take everything away
Until all that is left is you.
Then take you away
And the abode of happiness
Reveals itself.

*****

At all times,
There have been
Good people
Doing what they thought
They should do.
At all times,
There have been
Evil people
Doing what they thought
They should do.
This is the nature of the world.
There is no such thing
As a one sided coin.

*****

Those with wakefulness have lost everything.
Therefore, they have nothing left to lose.
They are fearless
In the face of whatever appears.

The process of Understanding is like
Washing a printed cloth.
First the design fades,
Next the background,
Until all that remains is
Plain white.
What began as white returns
To where it began.

*****

My dear children,
You are not
What you think you are
This what-you-think-you-are is
A shadow of
What you are,
Just as the moon
Reflecting on the lake water is
Not the moon.

*****

A thing can become spiritual
In any moment that
Its reference point is
Its Ground.

*****

Desiring nothing,
Disdaining nothing,
One cannot be impacted and is unassailable.

You come to Wu Hsin and ask,
 "Can you take away
My pain?
Can you take away
My unhappiness?
Can you take away
My fears?"
Wu Hsin cannot take away
Pain
Nor unhappiness,
Nor fear.
Wu Hsin can only take away
"My".
In so doing,
My pain
My unhappiness and
My fears evaporate

*****

I am dying
You are dying
It has been this way
Since birth.
To be free from death
Wu Hsin says
Look to what you were
Before this birth.

Man spends far too much time
Rejecting what does not suit him
But what does not suit today
May very well suit tomorrow
By then
It may be too late to retrieve it.
It is better to accept
All that comes
With deep understanding
That it is only temporary.

*****

If you knew this
To be only a dream
Would any of it
Really matter?

*****

Hearing with the ears is
Inferior to listening
With the heart.

*****

Love and compassion
Are natural
To the man
Lacking in
Self motivation.

To be,
No past or future is required.
These are requirements to be
Some thing in particular.
Giving up the lesser
Gains the greater.

*****

True loving must be pure,
Empty of all attributes.
It contains no I and
No other.

*****

The entire world is
Merely a play
Performed on your stage while
You are seated
In the front row.
Postscript:
Have no worries about
Being apart from Wu Hsin.
Wu Hsin is not leaving.
Wu Hsin is not going away.
Where would Wu Hsin go?
Never not here,
Wu Hsin is Now
Here
Always.

Translations of Wu Hsin by Roy Melvyn

Made in United States
North Haven, CT
22 November 2021

11391793R00085